Tb

Tony Boxell
30/1/95

THE
Long Road
Home

Eric Trethewey

Eric Trethewey

For Tony —

Hello again on the
long road *home*.

Rick

GOOSE LANE

© Eric Trethewey, 1994.

All rights reserved. No part of this publication may be reproduced, stored in a retrieval system or transmitted, in any form or by any means, without the prior written permission of the publisher or, in case of photocopying or other reprographic copying, a licence from the Canadian Reprography Collective.

Published by Goose Lane Editions with the assistance of the Canada Council, 1994.

Cover photograph by Allan J. Lee, 1992. Reproduced with permission of the artist.
Book design by Brenda Berry.
Printed and bound in Canada by The Tribune Press.

10   9   8   7   6   5   4   3   2

Canadian Cataloguing in Publication Data
Trethewey, Eric, 1943-

    The long road home

    Poems.
    ISBN 0-86492-178-0

I. Title.
PS8589.R5L66 1994   C811 .54   C94-950068-2
PR9199.3.T66L66 1994

Goose Lane Editions
469 King Street
Fredericton, New Brunswick
Canada E3B 1E5

*This book is for
Sherry and Cathy,
Joy and Steve*

Contents

11 Out in the World Enough: An Introduction,
    by David Adams Richards

I/ Leaving Suva

19 Prospective
20 The Text of Evening
22 Homesteading
25 The Tenant Farmer Conducts a Tour
27 '52 Pickup
29 Green Cadillac
30 Room & Board
31 Moncton Satori
33 Trains
34 Resurrection at West Lake
36 Leaving Suva, 1967

II/ Down A Familiar Street

41 Evening Shift
43 August Tableau
45 Soup
46 Consolation from a Woman of the People
48 Interlude

49 The Warship in the Channel
51 Foolish Questions Overlooking the Gulf
52 After Holding Out
53 Intercession at All Hallows
55 Wait
57 Down a Familiar Street
58 Postbellum
59 Lost
60 Stacking

III/ A Brief History of the Ironic Mode

63 The Man Who Smiles
65 The Wave
67 Irony in the Teaching of *Oedipus Tyrannus*
69 A Brief History of the Ironic Mode
70 Second Sight
71 A New Start
72 Wingtips
73 Versions
74 Night Driving

IV/ Reconnaissance

77 Reconnaissance
78 Poem at the Edge of Woods
79 Proper Reserve

80	Tom Thomson, Trees, etc.
82	Blind Lake
83	Blueberry
85	Hawks
86	Watching
87	Leaf
88	Waking at the Mount Olive Baptist Church
91	Walking Home
92	The Cellar

V/At Home

97	Ditch
98	Stillborn
99	The Colours
100	Hell on Wheels
101	Leaping to Conclusions
102	A Student Speaks of Companions
104	At Home
106	Evening Walk
107	Near Dawn
108	The Beautiful Rooms
110	Florilegium
111	Reading the Signs
113	Reading
115	The Long Road Home
119	Acknowledgements

Out in the World Enough

It is significant that within a year of Alden Nowlan's poems being introduced into the United States, the poems of Eric Trethewey will finally become available in Canada.

For these poets were born close to each other: both are Nova Scotians by birth; both often write about the hard scrub areas of that province's Rawdon Hills, about the area near Stanley, about the small farms, about the beauty of the cold and meagre earth they called home. About a world shadowed by poverty and violence.

And intellectually and emotionally, Trethewey is the most gifted poet to come out of the Maritimes since Nowlan. The empathy of both men comes from their vast lived experience. Both are as much poets of intent as they are poets of observation. (That is, the poet as a participant must have a say in matters of the world.) And both bring to their poetry an intensity of understanding, of lived thought and emotion that poets of observation have often failed to deliver, or, worse, are incapable of or frightened to acknowledge. Finally, both also know that the question of truth is moral in implication, without being dogmatic in presentation, and never merely clever in intonation.

Trethewey has the voice of a poet who has travelled most of his life: he lives in the United States and now teaches at Hollins College in Virginia. A number of his poems deal with the States, with people he has known and loved there.

But still his remains a uniquely Canadian and essentially Maritime voice. For this is his home, and he loves it, hates it, as do those of us attached to it by blood. In many of these poems he draws on his Canadian experience, from working small dead-end jobs in places like Moncton or Antigonish, to being a naval officer on a Canadian destroyer, to picking blueberries as a child in his native Hants County.

These are poems that chronicle a search — a search for dignity and a search for peace. A search that begins with an embittered boy and continues into the poet's adult life.

In "Homesteading," Trethewey writes about his grandfather who each month takes his family on a Sunday drive into the Rawdon hills, trying to find a place they can afford to buy:

> ... three generations of us
> gone from home, we bounced up the lane
> to the yard where chickens once pecked,
> dieseled to a stop by the greyboard house.
> There were sheds, a sagging barn,
> stony pastures skirted by acres
> of blowdown and raspberry tangle.

We find out it is a dream never to be. And as the poet walks to the stream below the house, he notices a heron and comments:

> And then I saw it, a long-legged stillness
> in the moving water, neck like a crooked stick,
> hunger gleaming in its jewelled eye.
> A band of last light flinty on the blackness
> spread flat between us, I stood there
> watching, wanting only this vigil
> above fish or whatever its head
> darted down to, once, and once again,
> this creature that knew what it was looking for
> and where to go to find it.

The farm is never bought. So it becomes a symbol of all things sought. More significant for the poet, and for us.

Trethewey's poems assert themselves in the same way some of Conrad's stories do. In these poems Trethewey is sometimes Marlow, often Lord Jim. The poems are fascinating because they are telling us of a life's journey: the self-made self of a man. A journey from Halifax to New Orleans and back again by a man who has seen violence and has grappled with real poverty but is never diminished by it. As he writes in "Consolation from a Woman of the People":

> We've retreated to Halifax
> in late summer, falling back in stages
> from New Orleans, all the way
> to here, the place I've been leaving
> all my life.

Strangely, these lines, written like notes by a field officer on a failed campaign, are victorious in a way poems of lesser weight, about happier things, can never be.

Like some of Conrad's heroes he has come through the struggle to tell those of us on either side about it, with beauty and pathos and humour.

Because it is a battle not all of us would be capable of entering.

So they are imaginative poems. But they are also strikingly, absolutely real. Often haunting, and more powerful than many things written today — as are the heart-rending and tender poems to Trethewey's murdered first wife.

In the poem "The Cellar," his wife comes back in a dream to remind us of the tragic waste of time, and of precious moments between the living that should never be passed over:

> *Let me in*, she mouths against the wind,
> and I try to, but the front door
> won't open, and when I hurry around
> to the kitchen, I hear a sob
> behind me — as if she thinks I'm turning

away from her. *Please let me in, I only want to say goodbye one last time.*

When Trethewey writes of something you know it has happened to him, to those closest to him. Blood and hope, anguish and surprise flow out of these poems, out of himself, out of those he knows and loves.

It is fashionable to talk about poverty, violence, and victimization. It is not fashionable to have to live it.

It is also, I think, fashionable to misconstrue, embellish, and misunderstand the truths these conditions can sow in the heart.

Trethewey has lived them, seen them in others, and so, being honour-bred, refuses to pretend to misunderstand.

He never goes for chortling, disingenuous sympathies. (He would, I'm sure, have gained more popular attention sooner if he had.)

In his earlier book of poetry, *Evening Knowledge*, Trethewey published the poem "In the Kitchen." The subject is an evening spent drinking with his stepfather, a man who has spent half his life foggily perpetrating violence against those around him. Not once in this remarkable, searing poem is the past reduced.

Though this man has committed acts against the poet's family that would turn most pale, he is shown in complexity and compassion. Taken altogether, the poem has something bordering on forgiveness and love — without once flinching from the understanding that violence could erupt again in a second.

Only those who have lived such an experience could write a poem of such humanity.

I will also never hesitate to say that these poems have something more; they have a constant understanding of the subtle motions of humanity, the dreams and tender motives of men and women that never much see the light of day, in a world that constantly tries to reduce human feeling. A world that unknowingly pushes us back upon ourselves, until we can no longer reach out to assist those we most care for.

Trethewey has seen all of that. He has seen that which reduces human feeling.

He has been out in the world enough. He has seen what tries to defeat us. He has stared it right in the face.

These poems are his spiritual answer, a reminder to us that human beings will reach towards each other.

And at our best, to those calling for our assistance, in whatever despair or hope, we will always answer.

> David Adams Richards
> April 1994

I/ Leaving Suva

Prospective

The houses, our houses, were huge
then, mystery stacked in their back rooms
and closets, the horizon made simple

by distance. It was summer, it was
everything quick with fragrance,
and we were like children

who believe without thinking
that when they come to the end
of a field, they'll be able to touch
the sky with their hands.

The Text of Evening

Suppose, for instance,
in that one spangled pause
of day's final sentence — lilacs
persistent as the must of old books —
a trout should flash above water
and hang an instant in the dusk
like some unsponsored meaning
teased from black pools of print.

Sentiments rich in uncertainty,
in promise,
may swoop like nighthawks
through the numinous air,
or cut across time's clear current
like the voices of children
belling over the damp grass
and under the looming trees.

Even so, even
if the twitterings of roosting birds
should come out of those trees
almost intelligible, almost
like the voice of Hermes,
what will they mean after all,
what alter or fulfil?

Trout back on the underside
of evening, small bells
stilled into silence, into sleep,
and birds settled mute in the leaves,
lights along the country road will open
one by one — flickering moments
held stolidly in place
like words in line on a page.

Homesteading

Once, driving the dirt road
that cut straight across the Rawdon hills,
the grade ahead a red slash rising steep
through the afternoon, we stopped
at an old place off to the left.
Maybe this time it would be the right one,
the one he was always looking for
in the newspaper or out along those country
roads — whose ruin he could rectify.
Whose price he could afford.

It was late, just before dusk.
Like a family, three generations of us
gone from home, we bounced up the lane
to the yard where chickens once pecked,
dieseled to a stop by the greyboard house.
There were sheds, a sagging barn,
stony pastures skirted by acres
of blowdown and raspberry tangle.

"Ain't she a humdinger?" Granddad said,
no more than a sliver of irony in his tone.
Fireflies pulsed in the long grass
around the place as he pointed out
this and that to Nan and Mom, how short
a walk it was to the well, the file

of alders below the house that told us
there was water on the property,
or how he might put running water
in the kitchen. At the very least.

My sisters fussed in the back seat
of that old Ford coupe of his he'd bought
cheap, thoroughly used since '48.
They were cranky, worn out from hanging
onto the hand straps down every back road
in Hants County, through every clutch
of houses with a name — Ardoise, Stanley,
Shubenacadie — learning no more than the landscape
of failure, abandoned farms leaning into hillsides
or settling to earth in a grove of dead elms.

Nothing better to do, I wandered
down to the water, followed its windings
into the trees, picking up stones
from the current to hold the comfort
of smooth edges in my palms, taken in by flashes
of fish, leaves jittery with wind,
what was left of the light.

And then I saw it, a long-legged stillness
in the moving water, neck like a crooked stick,
hunger gleaming in its jewelled eye.
A band of last light flinty on the blackness
spread flat between us, I stood there

watching, wanting only this vigil
above fish or whatever its head
darted down to, once, and once again,
this creature that knew what it was looking for
and where to go to find it.

The Tenant Farmer Conducts a Tour

Camp Inspectors. That's what they were called
in the lumber woods when you were young.
Because they didn't stay long, was what you said.
The one who came by bus that summer I was nine
swore he had worked on farms before — grew up on one,
matter of fact. So you showed him
around the place, in spite of that shirt of his
with the silver speckles, and those pointy-toed shoes
he stepped around muck in —
just to let him know what he'd have to do
if he got the job. When you asked him had he worked

with cows, he sniffed as if to say what he didn't know
about them wasn't worth a grown man's time
in asking silly questions. This, so he said,
was just the kind of place he was going to buy, himself,
eventually. In the barn at milking time,
you showed him the thirty head. And thirty bodies
you leaned your head against twice a day. Pointed out
some other odds and ends. It was August still,
the grazing lush, and we both saw that lifted
tail, that certain spinal arch — in time

to sidle left and right. Eyes on something
else, he stood there until it hit him square,

that semisolid aromatic spray.
Knowing his thin slouch for what it was,
you glared my grinning down, made me show him
the pump, help him sponge off his pants
while you went to fetch something from the house
for this stranger who needed work he couldn't do,
who would climb aboard the bus in your old blue shirt,
on the move, one more inspection tour complete.

'52 Pickup

Down at the General Store
he told us how
he'd bought it —
a half-ton Ford, 1952 —
in town.

It stood there
all shiny black
and primer paint
as he explained
how he would do the valves
and rings himself,
just as he'd tuned it —
plugs and points,
coil and condenser —
to say nothing
of the new battery
and the five whitewall radials
that nobody needed
to mention.

Saturday, he said,
a man he knew
would rebuild the carburetor,
cheap,
and a paint job

was in the works.
He said he'd bought
a *great* truck
and was fixing it up.

Someone else said
he hadn't bought
nothin'
but a game of cards.

Green Cadillac

Mornings we hold on for noon,
for sandwiches, cold drinks,
moments to take a look
at the landscape, or water
glinting in the distance,
remote as the feeling
of someone else's dream.

The afternoons have waited
for us all our lives:
a young woman, alone,
passing in a green Cadillac
along this slash of asphalt
dividing woods and blue water;
the horny talk of bored
and lonely men — who all need
the work. But if it rained
no one would care.

There are days when it won't
end, the body pulling
from daylight into dusk
through the dissonance of machines
and the sun's glare on hot tar,
acrid hours shimmering in the distance,
strung out ahead
flat as rolled pavement.

Room & Board

For three weeks now he has wakened
in this strange bed, this room
with flowered wallpaper, its tones
of pink and green that seem designed
to stifle appetite — to remind all
who pass through here of loathing
for the self, its intimate feel.
As he pulls on Levi's, laces up
his boots, asphalt caked on the soles,
he knows already what the day will bring,
and he hobbles down the hall
to the bathroom, breathes again
the rank bite of old piss.
The woman in the kitchen has been up
for an hour — he has heard her moving.
Her life depends on him and others
like him, though he has never seen her
before this month. Three times today
he'll eat her bland food, and when
evening has towed him back from labour
he'll sit on her steps in dusk's
sweet ache — until blackflies drive him
in to bed — and listen to the rasp
dried burdock makes in flutters
of breeze. For no reason he knows
he'll count first glimmerings one by one,
those heartbreaking beacons blazing.

Moncton Satori

By a grey house
on Bonaccord Street,
I come from the cave
of an ancient dream
amazed to see
red leaves falling.

Now, as one leaf flutters
on a hydrant nut before me,
somewhere in Asia
machine-guns rattle a rhythm
for clacking teletypes
a world away:
a young girl smiles
and gets off a Greyhound bus
in Bowling Green.

Somewhere to the south
of this old house
republics topple;
everywhere
ambitious public men
study the manipulation
of desire.

Invisible spheres wheel
through a boundless sky
while here, solitary,
standing by a grey house
on Bonaccord,
I watch
the red leaves falling.

Trains

If a child parses fields, counts horses
passing in the sigh of a summer afternoon
until night doubles windows into mirrors,
the moon will hang over the tunnel of his sleep;

and those fields lifting into a boy's dreams
may send him reeling back through cars, through
clacking couplings toward a stop left far behind.
The same moon will hover above the rails

for a man embarked on a later train
out of stations ringed by brick and iron.
Shoulders hunched in the cold, he will mourn
departures to the litany of wheels,

cities asprawl under blank winter trees.

Resurrection at West Lake

Ringed by dark palisades
of spruce and this cold, black
bowl of water, I understand again
about words, how folded wings

can open, lift into flight:
love, when it batters us,
or *death*, when we sense its swoop,
a wendigo stirring in shadows.

This one-crow sky leans on my bowels.
My eyes are admonished
by witch fingers of naked poplars
forming their mute adjurations.

And social voices fall silent too:
crows, chickadees, whiskeyjacks
contain their clatter; squirrels
grow mute as pinecones.

Up on the ridge behind me
thin, bone-white remnants
of the deepest snowdrifts glow,
skeletal under the hackmatacks.

Out of these enigmatic evergreens,
around imponderable granite mounds,
beneath one flapping black rag
of crow, time's surge begins again.

Leaving Suva, 1967

Crapulous beneath starched whites,
we are at the end of something.
Gangway up, official farewell
party gone, we perform
our final ritual: hoist
the whaler, reel the hawsers.

Off our starboard bow
a lumpish tug wallows by,
and the oiled ripples of her wake
flap at our stately hull.
Even the French minesweeper
tied up in the berth ahead,
tricolour slapping at her stern,
appears plain, ungainly
in our sleek, grey,
Canadian presence.

And above the harbour in the haze
the bulging hills of Viti Levu
rise, shield in morning shadow
a lugger limping home
to this inlet of the dispossessed.
Expanse turns its movement
to a still spot on the bay.

Their disorder
is accumulated early on the jetty:
several Indians, two Chinese,
a white New Zealand clerk.
Craggy-featured Fiji Islanders
sprung from the old spirits
of Nakauvandra
stand in groups and perch
on bollards, waiting, impassive.
We can see them gathered
in a frayed knot of flesh,
the girls from the Gala Guest House:
Rachel, Oona, heavy Naronga.
Are they touched by our frail
decorum? Curious about the inside
of this strange word *Canada*?
I hear only the creak of smacks,
the chafe and groan of the docks.
The odour of creosote hangs
on the air.

The innocence is gone.
Ordinary Seamen who have drunk
yangkona, who will leave
their legacy of bastards,
wear their whore blossoms uncertainly,
like new badges.
As we stand on our scrubbed decks,

engines going astern,
their backs are turned
to the graves of ancestors,
the old life rotting like fruit
in the street vendors' stalls.

Rachel's and Naronga's waving arms
are the wings of a great bird.
Is there a dream woven
in this shuttling of hands?
The destroyer comes around,
and we continue our centennial cruise

as Suva slopes and shimmers astern,
famished wishes gliding like gulls
after our carrion vanities.

II/*Down A Familiar Street*

Evening Shift

Approaching the evening shift —
springtime, New Orleans —
the bus crammed with lives
all leaning away from labour
toward a sense of what some things
are really worth: quiet rooms,
or cold beers on the steps
while children play in dwindling light.

*

Between rows of trucks
they sit on crates,
waiting for the man to take
their cards and point
to a van ass-ended up to the dock.
They know the rest by heart:
set up the rollers, roll
out the trollies, hump
crates toward distant dawn.
Wizened Art with his skinny arms
and Julio behind his mustaches
have learned to accept
this daily bread.

*

Past midnight, ten, twenty
years deep in it, they yank
at time boxed up into hours,
heaved onto rollers and stacked
in the holds of eighteen-wheelers
to be hauled away to places
they've never been to,
will never go.

August Tableau

They have detached themselves from the blue car
to stand at the meadow's edge
where a flood of perjured light attests
that their presence is entire.

※

There is no way to know
that in another moment
something will draw her out into the tall grass,
away from the man who stands facing her
and the striped kitten
moving in the grass between them,

or that she will turn back soon —
toward it, toward him —
and walk where the churchyard fence
borders bleached markers
littering like bones the mounded earth.

※

Now, in this seizure of light,
before movement begins again,
neither man nor woman knows
what can be carried away from here

or what will vanish down the road
when light collapses on the water,

or that long before then a solitary crow
will drift across the evening.
Its single, hollow caw
will jar this August into autumn,
call back bounty from the turning year.

Soup

The weeks come, windy, wet,
in which there is no work,
and the old woman simmers

potato soup, to feed us
when we come out of the woods
to her warm kitchen.

I mention another job in town
I didn't get, and she stirs the soup
as if I hadn't spoken.

We are the people, she says,
tasting it, her tone telling me
how this entitles us to nothing.

Consolation from a Woman of the People

When the striped kitten you adopted
in Vermont disappears,
we walk through elm-shadowed streets
and call into cindered alleys
Hard Times, Hard Times,
until our voices come back hollow
across the evening
and we circle home empty-handed
to sit on the steps
and watch fog roll in
off the black Atlantic.

We've retreated to Halifax
in late summer, falling back in stages
from New Orleans, all the way
to here, the place I've been leaving
all my life. Days of looking
for work and somewhere to live
have left us jobless, low
on cash, camped in at my mother's house
waiting for the fabled turn of luck.

We sit on the steps in silence
as the street lights come on,
and Kate, my widowed grandmother,
tipsy tonight on sherry,

appears in the doorway behind us.
Resting her hand on your shoulder,
she speaks in her old-fashioned way.
Don't you grieve now, Patty,
she says, *hard times*
always comes home.

Interlude

On the porch, crosshatched
by slatted sunlight,
we feel its warmth
in the wavering grain

and in these words
passed back and forth between us
like old coins with faces worn
from last year, years gone.

Nets of cloud
drifting in from the west
trail past —
afterthoughts almost,

like the first spattering drops,
the poplar leaves turning up
and flashing in wind,
one for every hidden grief.

The Warship in the Channel

My eyes open on a gull's high sail and swoop
over distant rocks and surf. A bruised sky bends
away on the pleated ocean; and a loop
of shingle winds around to westward, ends
at the burnished hinge of earth and air. The group
below us mime a grace that none intends.
Now, all things gather in this falling light
to plenitude, hard-edged to stay the night.

On this hill I've surfaced from a windy dream
of loss, of old names floating up from the dark
waters of sleep. Awake, I see we're abeam
of a ship below on the bay, perhaps a mark
on her navigator's chart. To him we'll mean
at the right degree to wheel to port, embark
on the fierce, estranging sea. Gulls veer and whip
on wind across the riptide to the ship.

Citadel and wallowing ship are bound
in destinies, though distance gives a silent
cast — to baffle waking sense. No sound
betrays the frothing surf; nothing is sent
from the ship to tell of her estate. Around
her bows the spume is folded like a tent.
Last light warms us on this privileged ground,
at peace above a wrangling sea of sound.

For chaos breaks below us on the bay.
Behind the mask that beauty wears, a sleek
destroyer lofted on swells, shrouded in spray
on a distant, heavy sea, there's the groan and creak
of bulkheads, sounds that have made some pray
for strength, and shuddering yaws to try the weak.
We speak of how old seadogs, lacking tables
can set a course, charm truth from old sea fables.

Foolish Questions Overlooking the Gulf

Why is distant water mostly blue,

or the ocean — blue, green or black —
laced with the sting of salt?

Why is that ancient abstraction *desire*,
like its objects, never at home in the flesh
but something always just beyond the real?

And why do dreams never end in the death
of the one who is dreaming, thrashing
into daylight, sweat-soaked, breathing
air still, to rise into the salt of another day?

What makes love the springtime of longing,
and why must we feel what is missing
in things as palpable as the touch of hands,
the press of bodies filmed with salty water
on a day in August, here, anywhere? Why?

After Holding Out

In an ashen light,
walking back over the shells to the house,
he shuffles a Phillips Petroleum statement,
a telephone bill,
and a subscription offer from *Time*,

thinks of his grandmother
out along those country roads
waiting for her life to happen,
for the one-armed mail carrier
to sidle up to the box in his dusty Ford
and give her a line on things.

Half an hour before he was due
he was always "late again,"
and half the time he billowed by
without even slowing down.

On certain days
she could make the chickens uneasy
just by standing in the kitchen doorway,

and he sympathized with them, he recalls.
What he needed then
didn't come in the mail.

Intercession at All Hallows

Here, in a cold, familiar house,
a crying infant in my arms
will not be pacified,
and three mewling kittens
are starving around my legs.

In time, I discover a way out,
through a sagging door and across acres
of burnt fields — familiar, yet strange,
like a half-remembered childhood room.

Circling a weathered barn,
I find my way into another house.
There is a kitchen, the smell of horses,
faces I have known across the years.
The child, knowing nothing of this,
continues to wail,
and the kittens have followed me,
only to be snarled at by a poodle
who will not let them eat
from a bowl on the floor.

Into this disorder
comes my dead grandfather,
washing his hands at the sink.
"Where have *you* been?"

my grandmother accuses.
He doesn't answer, looks
pleased with himself.
The tavern, I think,
when he begins to sing.

As his words come clear, she smiles
at the kittens under the table, eating.
In my arms I hold a laughing child.

Wait

Right off, I can see they're getting ready
to go away. It's evening again, after the chores,
and I sit with them in the kitchen, listening
hard as he launches another yarn, doing my best
to pretend that nothing at all has changed.
Stop it, Bill, you filthy pup, she hisses, blushing,
when he hikes her skirt as she passes near him.
Try some of this here slumgullion, she says,
setting a dipperful in front of me.
Her heart is so bad we can all hear it banging
in her chest like a worn engine rod.
Overall straps down, in his balbriggans,
he leans forward in that chair by the window
and the words begin. Soon, he can't quite catch
his breath, begins to snort and blow like a horse
just out of harness. Until he swallows a pill.
Howsumever, he says at last, as always,
ratcheting forward to lace up his boots.
This time, though, he stands up into uniform,
a limber young soldier who begins to dance.
How about some mincemeat pie? she asks.
From the deer we got last fall. By now,
she's highstepping too, four furious feet
rattling waterpails beside the sink, sloshing
water across the floor. So they slow down, glide
into a waltz across the kitchen as a fiddle

from another room scrapes out all but the words
of "Seamus O'Brien Why Don't You Come Home?"
The waves begin then, all the sad goodbyes,
and the two of them rise from the floor, drift
slowly out the window beyond the hem of light.
Wait! I'm trying to insist in tune to the fiddle,
just as a train whistle starts to tell the night
in another key what leaving means, swallowing
my thin voice. It doesn't matter. Even asleep,
I know what this is all about: the kitchen
has turned icy, night and snow blowing
through breached glass, a table bare as deal.
Like lowered flags, their old worn coats
and darned sweaters droop from nails
behind the cold cookstove. Everything they've left
me with is frayed, threadbare, cheap as love.

Down a Familiar Street

The temperature has dropped by half,
after weeks of tepid autumn days,

and we drive down a familiar street
past trees and houses we've known for years.

Since my recognition is no more than light
spread cold on the surface of things,

I remember a village, evenings in spring,
twilight silence blossoming into sound.

In the car it's warm. Outside, the live oaks
lean in wind. Knowing I'm lost,

I reach to touch your hand as you look up,
surprised by this change in the weather.

Postbellum

Conceding the futility of anger,
this wet morning settles in all the way —

a small mound of ashes at field's edge,
carried here from the house and dumped;

or the spang of metal, rage's dull echo
resounding here in leafless solitude.

Cows drift single file across the hillside,
rocking heads heading nowhere in particular,

and on a flat rock at my feet, a beetle
flipped upside down, legs soliciting

the air, agitates the gourd of its body,
wavering, however slightly, in place.

Lost

We headed north, whirled down east,
retreated south again,
scouting for the right signs —
it's all there
in the compass needle's homing swivel.

There were always trees, sometimes
hills, and the changing names
of rivers. Faces kept reappearing.
It might have seemed
that we were travelling in circles.

In those lost days
our wayward motions moved
alike in a dozen places.
Now they're on separate trails
gauging their singular ways home.

There is no map. We make smaller shifts,
allow for error, magnetic variation,
as we travel the winding miles,
conning true north,
still boxing the compass.

Stacking

It started with stovelengths of slabwood
armloaded into the shed,
tiered neat against the wall for winter.

Later, Sackville, Shubenacadie, somewhere,
there was hay to be pitched onto wagons,
then heaped high in mows for horses, cattle.

Fourteen, he worked the cut-off saw at the mill;
and when the deal-carrier, sweat-soaked and winded,
fell behind, he toted lumber too, stacked it

in piles. One thing leading to another,
he dollied cartons of caramel and maple creams,
almond nuts, every flavour, in a chocolate factory —

just about the way, years later, New Orleans,
he forklifted crates of wheels and rims, bolts
and gizmos to their proper warehouse tiers.

On the Gulf Coast, he packed boxes of bananas
into diesel rigs, humped sacks of ammonium phosphate,
slung them high in the hot holds of freighters

bound for India. Later, elsewhere, winter on schedule,
he turned to make out the years,
seasoned, stacked up like hardwood behind him.

III/A Brief History of the Ironic Mode

The Man Who Smiles

You never know when you'll meet him,
idling on a street corner
or walking jauntily along.
You don't know him, assume
he doesn't know you —
although when he turns away
from your glance, rapt in a private smile
that could teach the angels paranoia,
you begin to wonder.

Is he simply happy with the sky,
the sycamores cradled in coronas
of lemon-yellow light, air moving
on the sibilant tongues of leaves?
Or could it be the echo of some joke
he heard a day or two ago?

Not likely, you conclude.
There's a too-knowing cast to that smile
that doesn't try to hide
its superior acknowledgement of something
not quite right in your demeanour,
the thing you've always suspected yourself,
hoped no one else would discover.
And now, here it is, out in the open
between you. The smiler sidles by,

smug as a convert, eyes averted
out of delicacy for your shame.

But then he's gone, and you begin
to see that it's not nearly as bad
as you expected, now, finally,
that you've been found out.
And a new kind of smile infiltrates
your face as you stride along,
pleased to be prepared at last
to meet those who know the worst,
those confessors, dissemblers, deliverers,
those smilers of one-sided smiles.

The Wave

En route to interviews in New York
(at the MLA Convention) I pray for work
as I drive depressed through winter dusk.
The season's cut down to stalk and husk
through Pennsylvania, but up ahead
my eye catches colour, a flash of red

from an overpass connecting farm to farm
on either side of 81. An arm
seems upraised to me — in supplication
I think at first. But something in the motion
implies greeting instead — a harmless way
for a farmhand, bored, to pass a sullen day.

*

I don't wave back, though as reassurance
I would if there were the slightest chance
he'd see past my windshield's glare, lonely
as he seems, arm up, so neighbourly.
Or so I think until something spatters
across the glass in front of me, shatters

it into an opaque web, making me brake
in a slew to the shoulder, Sealand and Drake

Transfer blowing by me on the interstate.
Shaking by my car, enraged, I wait
for my heartbeat to slow. The waver, by now,
has vanished. The air smells a lot like cow.

✳

This polyglot lobby where the job search leads,
aswarm with spectacles, beards, and tweeds,
though not what we have come for, is always here,
repeating itself, as now, cocktails near,
we come and go, interviews done for the day.
Across the lobby, in a not unfriendly way,

someone waves. A gesture aimed at me?
I hesitate an instant. Then I see
it's the Chair with whom I interviewed
just two hours past. A nice man, I conclude,
returning his wave, hoping I'm correct,
not unwary now of what I might expect.

Irony in the Teaching of Oedipus Tyrannus

Outrageous? Certainly. That any man,
knowingly or not, should butcher father
at a lonely crossroads, marry mother,
breed upon her children and brethren.

It's a tale difficult to understand,
except, perhaps, for those who can't read
books and never feel the baffling need
to know truth on a page. For them, a damned

king is simply fact, and the gap between word
and flesh is the forgetting of acts long ago
in an old country. Still, the plot might echo
the daily grief by which they earn their bread.

Discovering *hubris*, those more literate
can point out precisely a *tyrant's* flaw,
indict him sure for what he couldn't know
and worse, the way he didn't know it.

Or, puzzling fate, they'll muse on why,
once announced, it can never be revoked.
(A matter of metaphysics they'll suspect.)
Stately in the pride of words, their high

sense of import in a phrase, some may take
longer than others to see the meaning
of ruthless disclosures concerning a king,
a noble man, if rash. For his parents' sake

and his own, he strove to avoid his fate
by relinquishing privilege: he left home,
riddled with a Sphinx. If he had known
what is only learned by living, of course too late,

he would not have had to reckon in arrears
for ignorance words may shield one from for years.

A Brief History of the Ironic Mode

> *Search into the depth of things:*
> *there, irony never descends.*
> — Rilke

Eventually, there may come a week,
then two, three, or more,
when the body elects to lie down
to prepare some future willing.

If at this late stage it rolls over,
considers rising to some occasion
a yard off in any direction, declines,
henceforth the way is clear

for new intentions to repeat themselves
like amusing anecdotes
while old notions, ungainly but persistent,
croak around the slackened form,

waiting to strip it down
to its white, ironic bones.

Second Sight

If we could all go back
in time, we wouldn't

be so content to let
things go as they did,

knowing how they'd turn
out, but shouldn't.

A New Start

In the sump of these nights when sleep
won't come, your mind a jittery lamp in a maze
without exit to the freewheeling dark,
you long to be able to shout "Enough!"
and step out of your weary body into another
past, announce with assurance a new start.

In the first bright morning of that new life,
dark circles vanished from beneath your eyes,
you will be seen by all who know you
as one pardoned, amazingly,
for what all, knowing the truth, would think
unpardonable. Your grace will prove a legend.

But back here, panicky in your circuits,
you know that even out of sleep you are dreaming:
there is no way but this one that leads you
against your will to where the mind, grown numb
with its twitch, settles into half-waking dreams,
circles toward dawn, skirting untroubled sleep.

Wingtips

Lost for most of the evening,
I end up here, know I'm here
to read my poems aloud — someone,
the host perhaps, has told me this.

Then why am I eating
my shoe? It's one of my old
wingtips, black, with pebbled
grain and a scuffed, filthy sole.

I should mind more than I seem to —
it's only the thought of where
this particular sole has stood
that has me slightly squeamish.

Otherwise, I'd be content to do
what something in the nature of now
demands of me, gnawing away
like a beaver at a poplar,

though this is tougher by a stretch.
And unlike the beaver, I don't
at this moment have an inkling
of why it needs to be done.

Versions

A crossing of the adverse dark
may in time come to crossing twice:
wallowing in turbid current,
sliding on wind-polished ice.

Night Driving

Amidst all these
designated turnings — exits, bypasses,
NO U TURNS — sometimes it may be best
to turn out of heavy traffic
where something in us
says we should, before
all the alternate turns
are seen and weighed.

And often we can gain time
travelling at night.
Then, on summer country roads,
pushing narrow cones of light
through the musical dark,
windows down, hearts open
to melodies austere
in their regard for simple truths,
we can study to avoid
the accomplished articulation
of wrong reasons
to justify or negate the things
we do or do not know —

a rich discipline
while travelling by night
to where we've never been.

IV/Reconnaissance

Reconnaissance

It is enough, at times,
if words do nothing more
than reconnoitre some old terrain —

what it's like to walk out
of sunlight flooding an open field
and into the shade of an elm,

where a rusted spigot
above a deal trough
drips water tasting of iron.

Poem at the Edge of Woods

where we have outdistanced the traffic's drone —
    the highway behind us a mile or more —
        and silence begins to be heard;

where our footfalls in bracken dog us
    like conscience and a shadow is more
        than a neutral absence of light;

where the leaves, when they quiver in tongues
    to the tug of air, will seem to insist
        on something, a right to be heard;

where all who listen will hear still voices
    murmur from a fault in the earth
        in a language older than words

Proper Reserve

Never, Hesiod counsels, step across
the clear water of rivers
until you first wash your hands in them,
then pray as you gaze into those flashings
or that stillness pooled between banks.

A friend to whom I show this passage
demurs at my reading of it, points out
that Hesiod says nothing of the need
to be holy in the presence of things
that precede our arrival: the earth,
its waters in their native purity.

And he nowhere implies that just
as water employs the slope of things
to consummate its ends, so we —
who are mostly water — must shape ourselves,
our lives by what the earth allows.

But he leaves no doubt for those
who dare to disregard a river's claims
that the gods will look hard at them
from behind those streams coiling
across the world, on fire at sunrise, sunset,
give them sorrow in time to come.

Tom Thomson, Trees, etc.

In dread of how certain landscapes
threaten always to exclude the human,
I've carried with me from childhood
your vision: drowned land, burnt forests,
the guiltless perfection of a northern river.

And those isolate trees
rooted there in bleak, unpeopled space,
where there are no words,
only the unspeakable language of light.

Here, green branches fill like sails,
small and forlorn before this westerly.
Whitecaps glint like knives,
thin-honed, steely arguments
pointing to some purely human imperative —
self-destruction more likely than renewal —
in those dark humps of silence to the north.

There, other limbs fall at an angle
across some slightly warmer line of thought
and seek out in their bony sag
a bearable notion of things.

The landscape, this wild north, relents
in time. Eventually it is necessary to see
how orange light gathers behind the jackpine,
ragged, rising up in shadow
like an old man at dusk.
Glimmers on the far hills
flank green water, brown earth,
rock, root, and branch
claimed for human space.

Blind Lake

Some morning in the pale first light
of dawn I will turn back and come upon the lake
unexpectedly, as a lost memory
steals back to the mind that lived it.

Between spruces wading out of the mist
I will go down again to the water's edge
and hear the creak of gear, the cadenced clunk
of oarlocks slinging echoes off the ridge.

Loons in the distance will laugh at the light
while trout rise like crooked fingers in air —
beckoning flashes to call someone back
to springtime, to himself in the dawn.

Blueberry

Genus Vaccinium, a field guide tells me
today, as browsing, I come upon the entry:
*Low to medium-sized shrubs
having rather small, thick leaves,
small, white urn-shaped flowers,
and small, round, many-seeded fruits
that are bluish when ripe.*

Then, a lifetime gone almost, we would
gather them in jars and dippers,
lard cans and water buckets.
Hot August days, we'd set out
for the barrens, or simply stop the truck
at roadside in likely places:
a burned-over strip, perhaps, where under
the film of road dust they'd be as brilliant
as a bluejay's bluest feather.
Or sometimes almost black.
I can hear yet the first *tock* of firm berries
against tin bottoms, each plucked globe
a memorial to the season's bounty.
As containers filled, there'd be leaf
and branch fragments, stems,
and little unripe berries green and hard
along with all the ripe ones, and no one
would mind much — though the younger you were,

the more you'd be scolded for careless picking
or putting more in your mouth than in your pail.
Boys would soon be shirtless, girls
stripped down to essentials. Once, in the bog
by West Lake, amidst summer's dry tick,
balsam fragrant around us, we spotted
a black bear up to the same thing
we were, though dressed still for winter.

Late in the day, back home, we'd all be sunburned,
sore, insect welts thick on our bodies,
lips and hands stained blue from berries.
Some of them we'd pour into baskets,
hold them aloft at roadside, for sale
to passing cars. And Mom would stew
what was left into preserves, or bake
in pies — often the same day — and we
would fake eating supper to get at them
sooner, hot and sweet, the thick juice
on our hands, faces, our clothes —
even our teeth would be blue
from this masterful pie, this rare pie
made from bountiful fruit, which, I'm reminded
by the field guide today, is *an important food
for bears and other forms of wildlife.*

Hawks

Those blots in the traceries of distant
sycamore and hackberry limbs raised black
against the December sky, seen up close
are birds, big-chested, scythe-beaked surveyors
of the ruck of daily life. Motionless,
they seem indifferent to the furtive prey
scratching beneath them through the hollow rasp
of winter.

       On the run, wary as fieldmice,
all day today we are hawk-spotters.
As we drive through Texas, Louisiana,
shucking off the used miles behind us,
we count them vigilantly north and south,
knuckled audacious on their tangled roosts,
arranged like destiny over the land.

Watching

When I stop the car to watch them,
they stop to watch me:
at the top of the rise, deer in the field —
one buck, a spikehorn, and two does.

The third day of hunting season.
Parked pickups line the country road,
their drivers tramping the woods.

But the deer are in this field,
and they are watching me.

Leaf

Because there are others,
we've made the long climb
into words, from that height
given names to all cattle,
to the birds of the air,
and to every beast of the field.

But when winter returns
and remaining leaves on an oak
tick against branches gone bare,
chiming the hollow of *leaf, leaf,*
other syllables are sounded as well —
of *good*, and *evil*, and *truth* —
old syllables recalling our grief.

Waking at the Mount Olive Baptist Church

Gwendolyn Turnbough, 1944-85

Our child, a woman now
almost, has made up her mind
to stand here at last and think *Goodbye*
over what remains of you.
Though I have told her
she should do this, when she sobs
beyond all seeing
there is nothing I can do but hold her
and lead her back outside
into what is left of summer light.

*

Twenty years. I've driven
through them all on the way here today,
each turning almost inevitable
considered from this side
of time. Old faces, once more
than faces to both of us,
have come back, drawn close
in a circle around you, their own.
Whatever marriage comes to —
a child in tears, beyond
all consolation, your body

laid out in cold attire —
has brought me back to witness this,
to fail not to see those marks
that make-up couldn't disguise
where bullets went in and out
of your temple, your slender neck.

※

That other husband of yours
who did this, for what
he fooled himself was love, desperate
love, ended what your mother began
back when she could still believe
in something that binds us
each to each, woman to man.
Weeping beside me in this pew,
she knows what else
she has lived for.

※

*In my Father's house
are many mansions,*
the minister reads, but what
can we bring ourselves
to pray for on this day?
Even the child you loved
like a better self,

led out of church at the sight
of what may be called love by some
can come to, is nothing to you now.
You are beyond us —
though there is something more
than the nothing we can give you at last
that needs to be held up in words.

Walking Home

Waking, I thought of her, six months
dead. It was that time of night.
I woke and thought of her,
an evening twenty years gone,
walking home up the long hill from town
we climbed so many times that year.

Nothing happened in particular,
that I recall. She wore a blue dress,
ruffles at the collar, and I carried —
I must have — this leather-bound book
they'd given me, the old couple
who asked us to dinner that evening.

The Poems of Robert Burns, an almost
forgotten kindness. They befriended us
when we were young in a strange place.
How could I not think of them, of her,
old time rising in the night?
How can I not, in wonder, repeat it?

The Cellar

Face at the window, her face
from years ago, out in the cold —
my long-dead wife, once wife,
snow blowing behind her, maelstrom
in the lower field. It's the old place
in Hants County, no more than a cellar hole
the last time I passed by.

Let me in, she mouths against the wind,
and I try to, but the front door
won't open, and when I hurry around
to the kitchen, I hear a sob
behind me — as if she thinks I'm turning
away from her. *Please let me in, I only
want to say goodbye one last time.*

Wailing with the wind, she keeps repeating
her grief as I run from door to window
to door, but nothing will open
to the need in her voice becoming
the need in my movements,
until it occurs to me at last —

the cellar. I pass through the pantry,
shelves stacked with preserves,
with the cracked china of childhood,

and lift the latch: this door opens easily,
as it always did, and the ancient smells
float up from below — rocks and ashes,
damp dirt, the must of generations —
and I step down the steep, narrow stairs,
feeling my way back in the dark,
calling out with each uncertain step,
Wait, please wait, I'm on my way.

V/At Home

Ditch

No more than a runnel
of brownish liquid, iridescent
with oil. Scum at the edge
where a wrapper of some sort —
red paper, blurred logo —
is half-submerged, bobbing
in the current, deeper now
than any meaning intended
by its makers. It reminds me
of empty cigarette packets
we scoured the roadside for
as boys, tramping
those rural miles, hoping
to find change, a large bill
from someone's pocket
wedged in a seam. And it's
the way I am still, on this day,
rain falling steadily,
and nothing, nothing at all to lift me.
On the bank, a cluster
of pale blue flowers
that I haven't noticed before,
can't name, rises up, holds
the light — how difficult
each day can be without
small gifts to brighten
our merely human lives.

Stillborn

When the song on the jukebox ends,
before someone feeds the slot again,
here's a voice to fill the moment
with its cheer: *My father hated
the sight of me*, it says. And who
can say exactly what it means?
*He put me in digs when I was twelve,
'prenticed me. And then I found
a factory job, worked until I married
and came to Canada.* It's the woman
down at the end of the bar, her story
in brief for anyone who cares
to overhear. *I've had five kids,
you know, two cesarean and three
of them stillborn*, she confesses
to the young sailor beside her.
I'm almost thirty now, she adds,
her tone almost a question, as if
to ask where this number points,
to some beginning that is hers
at last, or to her proper sum?

The Colours

The colours are awake in the kitchen,
though it's not at all what you might think.

Whatever is concealed in green is saying
cool, green things that want a tantrum of colour

brought under control. They want to subdue
the blue violence of cobalt beneath the glare

of heartless white. But green is a subtle weaver,
and subtlety is out of season.

Children, from a bedroom, can hear them,
these loud colours ready to stamp down

to a fleshy basement where a raucous red
will tattoo the walls and tap on the floor

beside the emerald phone sitting undisturbed
in a silence that nothing will break,
not even what is hidden in green.

Hell on Wheels

Long before skateboards were in,
he had one, moving with his own kind
of grace along tourist-thick streets,
knowing them well from a point of view
level with your crotch or the eyes
of staring, not-quite-believing children.

Although he is never obliged to walk
in them, he has an understanding
of shoes, impressed on him from sitting
where others spit and dogs shit,
wheeling from corner to corner, getting by
on what lands, heads or tails, in a tin cup.

Leaping to Conclusions

It will be winter, perhaps:
the streets, some wet morning,
in slicked-down light
and a dog, gaunt, limping
from house to house,
nosing through yesterday
mounded in plastic sacks.

If a man should appear,
making his habitual way
where brown grass protrudes,
insistent as the season,
from cracks in the smeared cement,
he may see that nothing has changed.
It will, in fact, be winter.

From nothing beyond these clues —
the smug lie of the houses,
the trees, bare beneath clouds —
will come the possibility
of a single gesture,
reassuring as a loaded gun,
conclusive as a leap.

A Student Speaks of Companions

It was noon, I was talking to a friend
when the soldiers came. For no reason
they beat me, put a hood over my head.
Not to know where we were going in the back
of that truck was frightening, or why
they stripped my clothes when we arrived.
They left me there for hours, blindfolded,
arms tied behind my back. And when
they returned, still no one spoke.
I was led out to another place, so silent
when we got there I could hear them breathing
all around as they strapped me
to a metal bedspring without a mattress —
the *toaster*, they called it — and turned
the current on. That wasn't all.
They used the *picana* too, bragging
that it was their invention, a new honour
for our country. All of them laughed
at the one who said this. They clamped
electrodes to my head, my scrotum,
screamed curses and beat me until I smelled
their sweat. I discovered that pain
can always increase, that always
there is someone willing to make it.
For months I was tied and blindfolded.
There was nothing to see, nothing to hear,

no one to talk with. Always there was
pain, even when the torture stopped —
mostly in my shoulders from being tied
so long. It was my only company. We waited
alone together every day for the next session.
Only once, for a short time, I was put
in a room with another, bound and gagged
like me. We communicated secretly
by clicking fingernails. It had
a simple meaning: you are not alone.

At Home

This morning, early, I wakened
to a knocking at the pane — an apple bough,
fruit-laden, stirred by wind —
and rose to the morning's clear gift.
Outdoors in sunlight, bending
to the kind of labour that gives back
more than it costs, I mowed the grass
and planted a sycamore that with luck
will rise above most things, outlast
all else I've set my hands to do.
Working this day to the nub, my own way,
I hoed the garden of its weeds,
the fragile order of an intention
added to what nature had to offer.
I took it. It was mine, though more
than most have reason to expect.

*

And now it is evening, late summer again,
light golden on the fields, a dark seam
of cloud above the mountain's spine.
The sky does indeed resemble a dome.
From the hill behind the house
where my walk has brought me, outcroppings
of stone on the slope below glow white

against the pasture's bottomless green,
outcroppings as we are of memory,
the daily bread of insult and affection.
Even here, away from others, an echo
of the evening news persists in mind,
that old tale of terrible things
that come to some who do, most who don't
deserve them. And I give back to the air
an old question: how to be at home
in good fortune on a rare day
in late summer, just before fall begins?

Evening Walk

Rising from a slough of stale thought,
I've climbed once again the tilt
of this stone-knobbed pasture.
Just beyond the sag of fence, a clutch
of toadstools glows in dusk-light
like tiny skulls, spindles of goldenrod
nodding above them, and somewhere nearby
a thrush's song slides like a caress
across the evening. Ambitious
as they have been all day for light,
the oaks around step backward into shadow,
while there on the valley's far side,
green cumuli of locust crowns float up
and over the ridge into other mysteries.
The stars, haphazard in their swarming,
blink on — remote, precise in themselves,
as though to pinpoint anew
the aim of each impossible longing.

Near Dawn

Tugged out of bed by a dream,
he enters the world, confronts
cats stalking the hallway,
aghast at this early walker.
The moon, almost full, glows
on the crust of old snow.

Back in the bedroom, his wife
dreams in a world that is his
to return to. Perhaps.
But for now he's here
by the window, moonlight
glazing the earth.

He is watching five foxes
drift through the yard, gather
for a moment by the pear tree,
sniffing the air, inquisitors
out in the cold. They turn to what
beckons higher up on the ridge.

The Beautiful Rooms

Early on a summer morning, cool,
the weather having changed overnight,
I'm here in this room at last, aware
of the acrid smell of the fireplace
recalling old fires. And within
that painting on the wall, another room
opens, spare and beautiful as well.

I can smell its cleanliness, almost,
bare wood floors, curtains billowed
before a window open to currents
of air that are palpable, nearly,
in spite of everything they are not —
though something of what is missing,
unreflected by the mirror in the painting,

is absent here too, incompletion
brought back in each surge of air
that riffles the curtains of this room
in which I sit before an emblem
of feeling, stately, all but anonymous.
Outside, birds insistently warble
some unspeakable plenitude in things,

while in here, all these makings
of unknown hands — furniture, painting,

the walls themselves — mime the gestures
of their dumb eloquence. Leaf-play
of shadow on the oak floor, on my hands
idle along these armrests. Licking
herself, the orange cat arches

for each difficult place — hamstring,
hock, ruff high on her back. The breeze
meanwhile has stilled; birds have subsided
to a distant occasional trill.
As the orange cat curls to a doze,
the day commences in earnest,
half-settled already into form.

Florilegium

Nodes of light on the table,
they glowed for almost a week,
daisies and asters and whatnot,
sensing in the air around them
noise of an alien tongue,
though living still in the language
of where they came from.

We gathered them one by one
by the side of the road,
up in rockhill pastures,
or down along the creek.
And we brought them here
to brighten habitation
with news of a fresher world.

Today they are stooping stems,
faces folding in on themselves.
Like the eye of day closing
at dusk, or the stars put out
by clouds, by heavy weather,
they are nothing to us now
but drying husks, their names.

Reading the Signs

Intent upon meaning, we mean
in time, as lovers do, to forge
our final sense of things.

But today we tramp along the creek
in search of local epiphanies
instead — moments so full of themselves
(green aureoles around their leaves)
no instant is left over for outcomes.

Though *now* always turns
into *then*: we know we'll arrive
at trees gaunt with November,
moments when nothing stalks up
to the edge of things,
each object abandoned to itself,
remote in hard-edged clarity.

This has a cold glory all its own,
though it doesn't last either,
complications unavoidably on the way —
such as what is offered down the road
in the glances strangers exchange

along busy streets,
the civil passage of untidy news.

Life speaks to us — all these little
things we are never done with.

Reading

Turning a book's leaves, one I've had for years,
an old book fragrant with time, I find
a photograph, for decades undisturbed.
Its creased and yellowed message to the air,
to now, has something to do with homelessness —
though the house in the photo is real enough,
as palpable at least as memory.
Once, before any of those who lived there then
knew where they were going, that poplar tree,
slender bole rising past the upstairs window,
put out each spring new leaves, vulnerable green,
to unfurl and later quake in the August air —
the same tree a boy might have spoken to
from his bedroom window some summer night,
his words no more than the season's uttered ache,
or that other nights he watered from the window
with his urine.

        Since then, long since that day
this photo was taken, in time forgotten,
I've been back there, walked across the field
to where the house once stood. Nothing was left
by then but a hole lined with rocks — the remains
of a fieldstone cellar — and the shaggy bole,
the brittle limbs of the poplar, almost dead,

but brandishing yet green flags for the season.
The hill the house had stood on — that too
was three-parts gone, bulldozed for fill, no doubt,
and hauled to some distant suburb. Not even
the worn-out implements, the broken toys
were things that I remembered from those days.

But here it is again, all here, an ambush
in the pages of a book, catching me out
in the pathos of that permanence we long for,
leaves with an annual green addressing the air.

The Long Road Home

When I look up, always I seem to see
myself as another who walks beside me,
a stranger I almost recognize, almost
am able to touch. And wherever we are, the way
is hard, steep and tortuous under the stars
where each traveller goes alone and each movement
made is a discipline to teach the grammar
of landscape and weather, intention and will,
of what and how to be. Once, back there,
it may have been an hour shy of dawn,
dirt road ahead and behind, the sounds
of birds twittering up another day.
Or was it twilight amidst rolling vistas,
escarpments of clouds stacked up against blue,
bottomless blue, when someone first set out
on this long road home?

                Backroad beauties
give way to interstates, interminable wastes,
north by northwest buffets by insane winds —
that happy life gone, all gone far behind him,
or still ahead at the end of an avenue
of gnarled but flourishing oaks. If not the will
of a god, what is time but endless turnings
turned on this road, this unforgiving road,

each step of the way worn smooth or rutted
by those who have toiled before? No standing still,
we are here with Heraclitus, air above
the roadway aquaver like roadworn hearts,
the shimmer of siren lakes off there ahead,
and phantasms of stubby evergreens, dry weeds,
wind-hollowed rocks stacked up at either hand.

Oh, the delirium of unconsidered journeys,
as we advance dragging our caravans,
all the dubious baggage we've taken from time.
And always there is winter waiting, winter
to contend with, the winter sky, and the grass
bleached at roadside as we lean into wind and snow —
the moon, the stars blanked out — gusts squalling
wild in our faces, sleet slicing our skin.
Is it any wonder we go astray,
give up too soon on the long road home?

Dear travellers, there is still to come that night,
beneath a blooded moon, and that furious thing,
hound or harpy, wheeling out of the dark, striking
against your legs so you stumble, fall perhaps.
Then, you'll hear it clearly, the tapping, the tap
tap tapping as the blind one shuffles toward you.
She comes from the archives of anguish, and blind
though she is, she knows you for what and who you are.
She comes with a gift that only you can value,

since only you know what its cost has been.
And she speaks, but only in a parable
that darkens what it foretells.

                      Then she is gone,
the one who remains left with what persists
of landscape and weather, and the cawing,
the raucous cawing of a single crow,
its counsel couched in uncanny, autumnal tones:
So much to be done, to be done, to be undone.

Acknowledgements

My thanks to the editors of the following publications in which a number of these poems, some in earlier versions, first appeared:

THE ANTIGONISH REVIEW: "Foolish Questions Overlooking the Gulf"; "Hell on Wheels"
APPALACHEE QUARTERLY: "Waking at the Mount Olive Baptist Church"
ARTEMIS: "Trains"; "Watching"
THE CANADIAN FORUM: "Tom Thomson, Trees, etc."; "Room & Board"; "Ditch"; "A Student Speaks of Companions"; "Second Sight"
THE CENTENNIAL REVIEW: "The Colours"
THE CHRISTIAN CENTURY: "Reading the Signs"
THE CHRISTIAN SCIENCE MONITOR: "Down a Familiar Street"; "Florilegium"
THE CHRONICLE OF HIGHER EDUCATION: "The Wave"
CROSSCURRENTS: "The Man Who Smiles"
CUMBERLAND POETRY REVIEW: "Walking Home"
THE DALHOUSIE REVIEW: "Resurrection at West Lake"; "The Warship in the Channel"
DEFFINED PROVIDENCE: "Proper Reserve"; "An Evening Walk"
DESCANT: "The Text of Evening"
THE FIDDLEHEAD: "Consolation from a Woman of the People"; "Soup"

FIRST THINGS: "At Home"; "Near Dawn"
THE HUMANIST IN CANADA: "Moncton Satori"
THE JOURNAL: "Irony in the Teaching of *Oedipus Tyrannus*"; "A Brief History of the Ironic Mode"
IMAGES: "Interlude"
THE LOUISVILLE REVIEW: "Leaping to Conclusions"
THE MALAHAT REVIEW: "After Holding Out"
MISSISSIPPI VALLEY REVIEW: "Postbellum"
THE NEW LAUREL REVIEW: "Night Driving"
THE NEW REPUBLIC: "The Cellar"
OUTERBRIDGE: "The Tenant Farmer Conducts a Tour"
POET & CRITIC: "Blueberry"
POET LORE: "Prospective"
POETRY: "Wait"
POETRY EAST: "Stillborn"
THE POETRY REVIEW: "Blind Lake"
POTTERSFIELD PORTFOLIO: "Green Cadillac"; "Hawks"
QUEEN'S QUARTERLY: "Leaving Suva, 1967"; "Evening Shift"
THE SEATTLE REVIEW: "The Beautiful Rooms"
THE SOUTH FLORIDA POETRY REVIEW: "Intercession at All Hallows"
SOUTHERN HUMANITIES REVIEW: "Lost"
SPECTRUM: "Reconnaissance"
SPIRIT: "Leaf"
THE TEXAS REVIEW: "Homesteading"
WAVES: "August Tableau"
WIND: "'52 Pickup"

YARROW: "A New Start"; "Poem at the Edge of the Woods"

"Florilegium," "Resurrection at West Lake," "Reading the Signs," and "Near Dawn" appeared in *Poems for a Small Planet: Contemporary Nature Poetry.* Ed. Robert Pack and Jay Parini, 1993.

"Wait" was the winner of the Cynthia Cahn/Anhinga Prize for Poetry, 1993.